Conversations with kids about topics that matter

Through Our Eyes

by Iffer Beisswenger, Margaret Eldred
and the Kids in Mrs. Reese's Class

Photographs by Jill Reese
Carolynne Krusi, Editor

Authorhouse
2007

AuthorHouse™
1663 Liberty Drive, Suite 200
Bloomington, IN 47403
www.authorhouse.com
Phone: 1-800-839-8640

First published by AuthorHouse 05/02/07

ISBN: 9781434313751

Library of Congress: Applied for.

Also by Iffer Beisswenger and Margaret Eldred:
The Way We See Things; Middleschoolers look at themselves and issues they face everyday. @2004

Printed in the United States of America
Bloomington, Indiana

This book is printed on acid-free paper.

authorHOUSE®

Dedication

To Jill Reese

Through Our Eyes is dedciated with love and appreciation to Jill Reese who has shown unsurpassed commitment to her students and to the field of education for thirty three years. Her classroom is alive with color, excitement and challenge, and she has passed on her sense of excellence and her enthusiasm for learning to generations of students. The authors of this book are among the many students who have thrived under her mentorship.

Acknowledgments

Through Our Eyes was made possible by generous grants from the Byrne Foundation and the Hyatt family.

Many thanks to the staff and the PTA of the Henry J. Kaiser, Jr. Elementary School for their assistance and support for the project.

Without Heidi Eldred's organizational and proof-reading skills and her ongoing enthusiasm, this book would not have been possible.

Thanks also to Paul for his endless patience and assistance, and to MarieElise Young for her help with typing and transcribing.

We appreciate the ongoing support and help from St. Paul's School and Deerfield Academy.

NOTE:

All royalties generated from the Authorhouse publication of **Through Our Eyes** go to the Jill Reese Creativity Fund to support the continuation of creative projects at the Kaiser School.

Table of Contents

Introduction
for Kids

By Iffer Beisswenger and Margaret Eldred

The transition from childhood to adulthood is an emotionally and physically complicated process. We are sure you have heard that plenty of times before. Part of the reason adolescence is so difficult for kids is because they are scared to talk about it. They avoid discussing changes with friends, siblings, and especially parents, at a time when these conversations are most needed.

Four years ago as middle schoolers, we decided to try communicating our thoughts through a book entitled **The Way We See Things**. We hoped that, if we started the conversations, others would follow. As it turned out, we heard from kids from all over the world who shared some of our concerns, and who were glad to know that they were not alone. Parents and teachers have also told us that the book created a way to start conversations with their kids.

We knew, though, that our perspective was limited to the view from our small New England town, so we were delighted to be invited to join the students from Mrs. Reese's class in Oakland, California to hear about their world. We have worked together to create **Through Our Eyes**, a book with a much wider and more diverse perspective and more voices. These kids have opened up to talk about everything from fun and friends to tough issues like puberty and death. If they can talk about these things, so can you. Once you get started talking, the grown-ups in your lives can make a big difference. But, only if you talk to them. It might be a little awkward now and then, but give them a chance. Tell them what you are thinking. We're guessing that, in the long run, you'll be glad that you did.

Introduction
for Grown Ups

Research has shown over and over again that ongoing positive relationships between youth and adults make a huge difference in adolescents' lives. Statistics confirm that these relationships are correlated with decreased drug use and smoking in youth, as well as increased school attendance and involvement in outside activities. Young people who have strong relationships with adults are also more likely to have positive attitudes toward school and more likely to go on to higher education. Not surprisingly, depression and loneliness are often decreased, and self-esteem increased as well.

The problem is that communication, which is at the root of positive relationships, often becomes harder and harder as adolescence sets in. It is challenging to know what matters to kids, and what is really on their minds. **Through Our Eyes** can serve as a catalyst for these important conversations. It is easier for young people to agree or disagree with an idea that someone else initiates than it is to bring it up themselves. Throughout the book, the young authors remind adults how important it is for them to set special time aside to listen to kids. It is often said that kids don't care what we know until they know that we care. Hopefully, this book will open doors for the conversations that let kids know how much you care.

Iffer attends St. Paul's School in Concord, New Hampshire, and Margaret attends Deerfield Academy in Deerfield, Massachusetts.

Kids' Advice to Grown Ups

Don't say no to kids too quickly.

Let kids spend lots of time outside.

Don't nag about homework. Offer help with homework, but after the question is answered, don't keep talking about why you are right.

Know what your kids are doing, but don't baby them.

See what vegetables your kids like and feed them those. Don't force them to eat the ones they hate. Don't make kids "clean their plates."

Spend time with kids individually, even if it is just to do errands.

Let kids be independent whenever possible. Let them have choices.

Let kids have occasional junk food and video games.

Never say, "I'm older than you, so you have to do what I say."

Do not pass down racism or prejudice.

Ask kids' opinions before signing them up for things.

Never insult or tease kids. Never embarrass, humiliate or disrespect them.

Don't be hypocritical and expect kids to do something you don't do. Follow your own rules. Take your own advice.

Don't get all red in the face when you talk with kids about sex. It makes it hard to talk.

Don't depend on kids for jobs that are too big for them to handle.

Explain how to do the chores you want kids to do.

Never hit or kick kids. Never swear or scream at them.

Start teaching kids manners when they are young. Manners are harder to learn when kids get older.

Spend plenty of family time.

Never discourage your kids.

Help kids to manage the number of activities and sports they are involved in so that they are active but not overwhelmed.

Be honest with kids.

Don't spoil them.

Don't smoke around kids.

Don't expect your kids to live your dreams. They have their own. They need your help and support to reach their goals.

Make sure kids have fun.

Friends

Margaret: My friends are some of the most important people in my life. What do you think makes a good friend?

Malcolm: Most of my friends are bright. Some of them are funny, and some of them are ghetto and crazy. All of my friends cover my back, and none of them would turn their back on me. If one of my friends crossed me, I wouldn't care. I'd find a new friend.

Tommy: Friendship is something easy to come by if you are friendly and easy to be with. I have a lot of friends, but, sometimes during different time periods, I'm closer to some friends than I am to others. For example, in our class we switch seats, which moves you away from some people and brings you closer to others. I think friends help you cope with difficult situations.

Yasmine: My friends are very funny. They are always telling jokes.

Nolan: My friends aren't the kind of people who make fun of people all the time; they are nice to people.

Marina: I have lots of friends young, old, and in between. I think a good friend is trustworthy, kind, fun to play with and someone you can talk to.

Richard: Friendship means that you have a someone who you can count on. I like having a few good friends. My friends are important to me because, without them, I would be lonely and not have anybody to hang out with.

Gabriel: Friends are people who you can spend time with that you don't feel threatened by and feel okay talking to. Friends are people who you don't need to count on. (You should only count on yourself.) They will give you their honest opinion about something. Friends are important; they are necessary.

Ella: I agree. Friendship is very important in my life. My friends keep me happy, and we always have fun together. They can cheer you up when you are down. You really get to know a little bit more about a friend each day. You should listen to them because they might have been in a similar situation and can give some very helpful advice. Being friends with someone is a commitment because you don't want to let them down.

Olivia: I think a good friend is someone who you can trust and who is truthful. If you had a friend who lied to you, then that wouldn't be good. I also like a friend who is funny. I like it when your friend tells you a joke, and then you crack up. Those are fun times. I only like to have a few good friends because if I had a huge group then somebody in the group might be a troublemaker. I think that my friends are cool, fun, funny and smart.

Sophia: Friendship means that you cannot break promises. You will be honest and always tell the truth. Keeping secrets is another important part of friendship.

Truman: That's true. A friend should always keep a secret unless it will hurt someone's future.

Darius: To me, friendship means that you know, trust and respect someone, and they feel the same about you.

Nicholas: Yes, those things, but also sharing the same interests, liking the same games and having honesty and courage are what make a good friend. One of my friends loaned me a wonderful book about cats. I read it from cover to cover.

Meaghan: I like most people I meet, but they are not as important to me as my closest friends.

Campbell: A friend helps you out and doesn't try to avoid you. Your friends are people who you go to when you're having trouble. If friends get in fights, they should be able to make up.

Neijah: I like my friends because I can go to their houses and play with them. When friends are hurt or feeling down, I usually talk to them and make them feel better.

Chardonnay: Good friends are always caring towards you. They support you and never leave you. That is exactly how my two best friends are who go to school with me. They are so loving. That's why they're my best friends.

Truman: Here are what my friends are like. They are all pretty much tall compared to me. They all have dark hair. They're really important to me because it's nice to have other people in your life besides your family. They're sort of like your cousins. Also, you don't need someone who is bossy and saying all of your imperfections all of the time.

Nick: If friends are constantly hurting you or lying, they should not be considered friends. Friends will help you, and they will know you for a long time. If you are not a good friend, you will hurt people, and that's not good.

Noah: A good friend is someone who keeps your back, and helps you when you are in trouble.

Iffer: What qualities in your friends make them good leaders?

Nicholas: Intelligence, helpfulness, fairness, bravery, and honesty are qualities that make good leaders.

12

Noah: A good leader is a person who always listens and is nice to other people; someone who can solve conflicts.

Marina: Yes. They listen to others, but also they have integrity, follow directions, and treat others fairly.

Truman: What makes good leaders is that they are stern and nice, but know when to draw the line. To me that's the number one thing. Then, that they are not too bossy. It really annoys me when bossy people are in charge. Last, they know how to get things done fast.

Campbell: My friends are good leaders because they are honest. They could not tell a lie to anybody. They are confident. When there is a chance, they always run for office. They get along with almost everyone, and they can solve problems without making anyone mad.

Nick: A good leader is trustworthy. and does not treat others in a bad way. They will help you and bring you to safety.

Chardonnay: About half of my friends are responsible, committed and trustworthy. I'm glad that they have these qualities because I don't want to have friends who always get into trouble or tell lies or talk back to adults.

Neijah: When someone tells them to do something bad, they won't do it, and they'll tell the person, "That's wrong!"

Margaret: What subjects do you talk about with your friends that you aren't likely to talk about with grown-ups?

Noah: We talk about conflicts between friends, personal things like having a girlfriend, and other things like sports.

Marina: Some of the things I talk about with my friends are how the math was really boring or how some teacher or person was annoying at school. Sometimes we talk about a certain TV show that was on last night.

Nick: Me, too. I talk about sports and friends to my friends. But I do not talk about anything else because I am still young right now. I talk about the sports that I do, like lion dancing and Kung Fu. They are hard, but they are really fun.

Nicholas: I talk to my friends about codes and toys.

Truman: My friends and I usually talk about things that are going on at school that happen during recess. Sometimes we talk about what people are saying, but we know a lot of it is not true.

Campbell: Nothing. There are no secrets or information that I would tell my friends that I would keep from my parents. If I can tell friends, there is no reason not to tell a grown-up, too.

Chardonnay: Well, we usually talk about music, middle school, and celebrities. Mostly, we talk about celebrities. There is one guy in particular who we talk about. We practically drool over him.

Iffer: What do you do when a friend lets you down?

Marina: I talk to my friend who I had a problem with, explain how she has let me down, and how my feelings were hurt. Then, I suggest a better thing to do next time, in the hope that she will understand and take my suggestions. I also hope that she doesn't take offense to what I've said or get mad.

Campbell: I am not really sure. I've never been let down by one of my friends. But if I were, and they did something really bad or mean, I would try to make new friends.

Truman: It never really happens much now, but it has before, and I didn't feel like talking to that person. It really is disappointing and makes you feel bad.

Neijah: When a friend lets me down, I don't start a fight. I just walk away, and I don't say anything. When you walk away, you let the other person calm down, so that when you do want to talk, they will be reasonable.

Chardonnay: I do the same thing. When my friends let me down, I simply walk away from it all. I find more friends to hang out with. If that person says "hi" to me, I say "hi" back, and I know that we can be friends again.

Nicholas: When my friends let me down, I feel sad because they can be really bad and get me in trouble. Sometimes they tell me something and don't do it, then lie to me. You can also get in a fight with your friends, and get really mad about it.. Sometimes it is normal. It just means that you are really good friends, and you can argue a little.

Noah: Just ignore the people and the friend who let you down and take some time away. If you decide that you want to be friends again, you can talk about the problem.

School

Iffer: What are the most fun things that you do at school?

Sophia: Talking and socializing with all my friends are probably the most fun things that I do at school. I really enjoy competing against my friends at school in chess. Competing in sports is also fun, but most of the time it is too frustrating. I absolutely love poetry and writing when we don't have an assigned project.

Nicholas: The most fun things to do at school are writing messages to my friends and teachers using my own code that I created, playing at recess, and reading.

Tommy: Recess is what almost everyone likes best. I also enjoy math because I do it incredibly fast and can finish all of my homework during class time. Physical Education is also fun because it gets your energy out.

Ella: That's true, and P.E. gives us a chance to play different sports games outside. I also like music class at school because of the group effort it takes to put the whole song together.

Nydesha: I like music, too, because it soothes my mind. One day I want to be a famous musician.

Marina: I like art because there are many different kinds, and it is easy for me. I also like logic games because everything fits together so well if they are done right. They are so fun.

Darius: I think the free time that we sometimes get during the day and at recess makes school special.

Iffer: What are the biggest challenges at school?

Nicholas: The hardest thing is trying not to over heat when teachers are yelling at me to do something I can't do.

Tommy: The most challenging thing is putting up with other kids. Being gracious and kind, but not fruity, is the toughest thing in school because you have to maintain it. There are some people who will always think that you are a jerk just because they have a different personality.

Nydesha: The biggest challenge for me is math. It confuses me because of the different way I learn.

Sophia: For some people, making friends is challinging, but for me, it's not talking in class. I am also challenged in spelling. Solving problems with others can be a challenge at times because people all talk at once, and they don't respect or listen to what you are saying.

Marina: My biggest challenges at school are reading and writing. These subjects challenge me because they take a long time. Sometimes when I don't know what to write, I sit down with one of my parents to talk about the writing, and then I write down the most helpful things.

Ella: Reading is very important, and I don't have trouble with it. I just don't like to do it. I read some things, but when we're supposed to read a chapter of a class book, it's boring. Some books I like to read, like non-fiction books. When people say what books they've loved, I can't really say much because I haven't read any books to share. Writing books is much more fun than reading.

Margaret: Why do you think some kids make the decision not to go to school anymore?

Nicholas: They don't like the bullies, they did not have success in their classes, or maybe they had to get a job to help support their families.

Ella: I think that they don't get good grades and give up on themselves, or they are distracted, maybe by smoking, drugs or things they think are more important. They don't want an education, or they don't think they can succeed.

Sophia: Some kids have children at young ages and can't afford to go to school. Some kids who get bad grades and don't understand what the teacher has assigned drop out of school.

Tommy: People quit because the bullies and morons just get to them, or they hate school. They just feel a lot more comfortable, and it is easier to be with people you know very well at home.

Nydesha: I agree with Tommy and Nicholas. Some people probably don't go to school anymore because of bullies, or possibly because they think they're not smart, even though they really are.

Marina: Sometimes students have difficulty with working in a classroom, and work better by themselves maybe because of a learning disability. Other times, it's because they are not getting along with other people at school.

Margaret: What opportunities do you think you will have if you stay in school that you wouldn't have if you quit?

Nydesha: You could get a lot of scholarship money for college.

Nicholas: The reasons to stay in school are to get a chance to go to college and get a good job.

Marina: Yeah. You could get a better job or career in the future, and you would have a chance to learn more. Some people don't go to college, but they can still make a good living. Other people who don't go to college get into crime and alcohol.

Ella: If I continue with school and do well, I will have the opportunities to own a nice home and have a good job that pays a lot of money. People who drop out won't be able to get as good a job to provide them (and maybe a family) with what they need. At the least, they won't be able to get as nice things. Everyday life may be harder without math, reading and all these school skills.

Sophia: I agree with Ella. I also think that a person who drops out of school might miss the opportunity to make many friends because he or she might be judged as not being smart and not working well with others.

Tommy: If you continue to go school while being friendly, you will have a few more opportunities. You might be able to take more subjects or meet more friends, but most importantly, staying in school hardens you. You won't have your feelings hurt so easily.

Iffer: What advice do you have for teachers?

Nicholas: Be kind and polite. Use a soft voice. Help kids stay on task in a nice way. Get rid of bullies. Like your job. Don't be absent because subs are awful!

Tommy: Don't let your kids' feelings get hurt as a teacher. The best advice I have for most teachers is just to listen to all of your kids. Don't just listen to the kids who can follow directions the best.

Ella: I agree with Nicholas. A teacher should stay calm with a troublemaker.

Marina: I think teachers should make lessons as fun as possible so students want to pay attention. Also, have a time for taking a break so students aren't too bored.

Sophia: Assigning the class the proper amount of homework is a great piece of advice. Many children do not like homework, and if a teacher passes out too much, that particular teacher is called mean. Kids are very candy motivated, so if you give a challenging math problem, you can reward all the right answers with a small piece of candy. Allow kids to have time to do their homework at school. Make sure that all your students know that you care about their problems. Notice if they are becoming bored and create a more entertaining way of working on the subject.

Nydesha: My advice to a teacher is to take your time and encourage kids to be the best they can be. Also, a teacher should always stay calm so that students don't get mad and off track.

Homework

Iffer: When I was younger, I thought that teachers shouldn't give homework at all. Now, although it still isn't always fun, I recognize that it is necessary to keep up with the material in my classes. What do you think is a reasonable amount of homework?

Campbell: I think that the amount of homework doesn't really matter as long as you don't do twenty different things in one night. I usually have fun homework, so it isn't that much of a problem.

Meaghan: I think that we have too much homework, but that's just me. I could probably do more, but I swim almost every day. It takes up lots of time, so it's kind of hard to do homework.

Gabriel: I agree. Teachers give out too much homework. I think that kids should have only three things for homework: math, reading, and writing.

Marina: I think homework is good, but when there is too much it's not so good. At the beginning of the year, I had a hard time getting it in on time, but as the year went on, it started getting better, a lot better. Even though homework helps you, I don't like it.

Margaret: What do you do if you need help with homework?

Isaiah: If I need help with my homework, I ask my parents. And if my mother can't help me, I wait until the next day and get help from my teacher at school.

Campbell: I usually ask my teacher, ask a parent, or I look it up on the computer. Otherwise, I just keep working at it until I find a way that it makes enough sense.

Gabriel: You can also ask a tutor. If you know a friend, you could ask him to come to your house and do homework together.

Meaghan: If I need help with my homework, I usually get a piece of scratch paper and try to work it out by myself. If I still don't get it, I ask my parents, and they explain it to me. If they don't get it, then we go on the Internet to research it. Sometimes if I don't get it, I go to bed, and when I wake up and think about it some more, then I get the answer.

Marina: I ask my teacher or my family. At home when I need math help, I usually ask my sister.

Learning Differences and Disabilities

Margaret: I have a learning disability, and I have to deal with it every day. It is hard when other people don't understand and make judgments. I always knew that I had a harder time accomplishing some things than some other kids. Finding out why was really helpful. Understanding my disability has allowed me to succeed. Do you think that most kids your age understand learning disabilities and different learning styles?

Richard: I don't think many kids my age understand learning disabilities and differences. Even people my parents' age don't understand them. They say, "Why can't you read?" and I say, "I'm dyslexic." They don't understand why I'm not already reading. They think if I just try harder that I will be able to read.

Savannah: I agree. Kids our age judge people by their appearances and how they do in school. I know a few people with learning disabilities, and they react a lot differently to things than I do.

Kristina: I think most kids our age know a lot about their problems. The kids with different learning styles know that they have the problem and have different kinds of approaches for solving their problems.

Tommy: Some kids think that they are better than kids with learning disabilities and think that it is okay to make fun of them. But this is not okay. Kids with learning differences didn't choose to have a disadvantage. They didn't choose to have a more difficult life.

Iffer: What kind of challenges do you think kids with learning disabilities have?

Richard: I have a lot of challenges because of my learning disabilities. One of the hardest things is that you don't learn to read until you are older than when most people learn.

Kristina: I think kids with learning disabilities have a hard time learning different things in classes. For example, one of my friends has a hard time paying attention. He draws which makes it easier for him to understand.

Savannah: They have to deal with people thinking they're weird because they do things differently from "normal" people. A lot of kids our age stereotype people like that. It is unfair that they judge people.

Tommy: They have more challenges than the majority of the population. Some people think they're idiots and cannot do anything. This is totally not true. Some people are savants and are geniuses at one thing.
One of the most difficult challenges is that people might not want to be friends with them.

Margaret: What can all kids do to make sure that kids with different learning styles have a chance to excel and enjoy school?

Richard: I would tell other kids not to make fun of kids with learning disabilities. Even if they can't read or if they learn differently, they are really just like you or your friend. They are sometimes smarter than you, but just not in reading.

Kristina: Richard is right. I think kids should not laugh at them, make fun of them, tease them, or call them names.

Savannah: No one should make fun of people who have learning disabilities. They can try to be a friend instead. If you see someone making fun of a person with learning disabilities, try to stop it.

Popularity

Iffer: In almost every school I've ever been to, there has been a "popular" group. Sometimes they have been my good friends, and sometimes they were the kind of people with whom I don't want to associate myself. What makes a kid popular at your school?

Nydesha: To me, being popular means that you are a very nice person, and that a lot of people want to be your friend. Also, being popular means that you are smart and can handle lots of things at school.

Karen: The popular kids at my school can sometimes be mean. They talk about people behind their backs and get in fights. They sometimes bully other kids. I like to hang out with a few people in the group, but I stay away from the others.

Chardonnay: Well, to be popular at my school you have to wear the best clothes, have the best hair, but you don't have to have the best grades. I may be referred to as "popular" at my school, but I'm not the snobby, perky, smart-alicky girl who always gets her way. I'm just plain and simple.

Truman: I'm not really sure because at school I don't think there exactly is a popular group. If there were, what would make them popular would be their clothes and their sunglasses and things like that.

Gabriel: I agree about clothes, and the way they talk and how many friends they have also make kids popular. Most of the time if they have cool clothes, they have to talk "cool" as well. Also, if they have friends that are popular, they are popular too.

Nikki: Well, there are different kinds of popularity. There are girls who always get the hottest boys, and there are people who just like you as a friend. I hang out with the popular girls because, when I first came to my school, there was a girl who was part of the "popular" group who toured me around. She is the nice kind of girl, but some girls are very mean. They might run for student body president or other offices.

Margaret: What are the negatives and positives about popularity?

Nydesha: A negative thing about popularity is that some people think they're better than everyone else. Positive things about being popular are that you get along with everybody, you have good grades and most people want to be your friend.

Truman: I think a negative thing about being popular is that everyone watches TV and knows that popular people are mean on TV, so they might assume that you are mean, too. That would be a big shame if you actually were a nice person. Also, being popular might start going to your head, and you might start acting all high and mighty. People might stop liking you. A positive about being popular is that most people in the school know your name. A lot of people want to be friends with you, which is a good thing if they are nice.

Karen: Sometimes the people in the popular group can be mean and talk about other people. On the other hand, some of the people can be nice. Even though the "popular" group often wears the latest clothes, they aren't rude. Sometimes the "popular" group is not so bad.

Nikki: That's true. Some people who are popular can be mean and can look at you in a very mean way, but some are very nice. Sometimes people trick you into doing things you do not want to do by saying, "You are going to be cool." But, you aren't going to be cool; they just want you to look like a fool.

Chardonnay: A positive thing about popularity is that if you've been neglected for most of your life, then you have the chance to get all the attention around yourself. A negative thing about popularity is that you can't change yourself if you wanted to. You always have to think about what your "popular" friends think. Also, you could become "less popular" if you act mean toward others.

Gabriel: Plus, even when you are in the "popular" group, some of the other "popular" people might not like you. And, there's the constant pressure of trying to be "cool". A positive thing is that you would probably have more friends.

29

Secrets and Rumors

Margaret: I know how awful I felt when a rumor was going around about me, and I couldn't figure out what to do about it. What is the difference between a secret and a rumor?

Truman: To me, a secret is something you tell to someone else, and they don't tell anyone unless they have to. A rumor is when you tell someone something, and they tell someone else, and then they tell someone else, and so on. After a while, lots of people will know the rumor, but the details will be changed, and the story will be different.

Richard: A rumor is likely not true and is spread from person to person. Usually, it is something negative about somebody or something that is going to happen. A secret is something that you don't want others talking about. When people find out that you have a secret, it makes them feel bad.

Alyssa: I agree. A secret is something that only a few people know about, and those few people aren't supposed to tell. If they start to tell other people and spread it around, then it becomes a rumor. Rumors can also start by people making something up and trying to spread it.

Karen: A secret is something that is very personal and usually kept private. A rumor is a lie about someone or something that spreads publicly.

30

No one likes a rumor to be spread, so try not to start one or be a part of it.

Yasmine: I think that the difference between rumors and secrets is that rumors are spread around when someone is mad, jealous, or just plain mean. Secrets are usually told to a best friend because you can count on best friends not to tell everybody. Secrets and rumors usually turn out the same at the end: someone gets hurt.

Iffer: How do you react to a rumor that you realized was hurtful to you or someone else?

Yasmine: I don't like to hear that a student's feelings have been hurt. I feel sad and upset when kids talk about other kids in an impolite way. Words can hurt. Think about what you say before words come out of your mouth.

Truman: If a rumor were hurting someone's reputation or feelings, I would tell an adult. Then they could take care of it, and hopefully, no one would be hurt. If it were going on about me, I would do the exact same thing: tell an adult.

Karen: I know when a secret has been told because people will not talk to you or avoid you. Here are two other ways to notice: One, they tend to be mean. Two, they might start hanging out with someone you don't like.

Richard: When I hear a rumor, I usually tell an adult, or tell the kid to stop spreading a rumor that is not true.

Alyssa: The thing that works best for me is to deal with the people who start the rumor. For a while, people were saying how some friends and I were excluding others from a game that we were playing. It wasn't true and made me upset because most of the people spreading the rumor didn't even ask to play with us. So, I went up to them and told them just to ask to join the game. They did, and soon there were a whole bunch of people playing.

Margaret: Do you think that there are times when a secret needs to be told to someone else?

Yasmine: A secret needs to be told when the secret is dangerous. An adult needs to be included in the situation so kids won't hurt themselves. For example, if the secret is about taking drugs, you need an adult to intervene.

Truman: I agree with Yasmine. Tell an adult rather than let a secret hurt someone, especially if that secret could ruin his or her future. For instance, if someone my age told me that she were pregnant, I would definitely want to tell an adult.

Richard: You have to tell an adult if it might affect someone' s life! Also, I would tell a teacher immediately if somebody were cheating on a test.

Iffer: When are secrets good, and when are they bad?

Alyssa: A secret is ok if you are telling your friend about yourself, but it is never good talking about someone else. If you have something you want to tell your friend, but not everyone else, you should wait until anyone close by leaves so that you don't hurt anyone's feelings.

Truman: Secrets can be good if you are telling someone something good about another person or yourself. They are bad when you say something nasty to a person who would tell other people, because it turns into a rumor.

Yasmine: I think that secrets are best when you keep them to yourself. Secrets are often bad when you tell everybody. The secret expands and changes.

Richard: But, secrets can be good if it is for something fantastic like a surprise party. It is when someone can be injured or their feelings hurt that secrets are bad.

Bullying

Iffer: I remember when I was younger, there was a guy on the bus who would say things to intimidate my friend. He would take my friend's hat and steal money from him. My friend felt really powerless, and it made me mad. Have you ever been bullied or seen other kids being bullied?

Ben: Most of the time bullies pick on people who are weak. I remember when I was younger, a bully forced a friend of mine to do his homework for him at recess. My friend was mad, but he didn't stop doing the work because the bully threatened to tell lies to the teacher about my friend. Sometimes the teacher even believed the bully's lies and kept my friend in from recess. Finally, the bully was expelled.

Sophia: Bullying doesn't always have to be physical to hurt someone. A few years ago, we had a new kid join our class. Most of my other classmates would not get near him because he learns differently. Then, a few kids began to start rumors that he had dangerous and contagious germs. Everyone has germs, and his germs were no different then ours! Because I was one of the few people who hung out with him, people said that we were boyfriend and girlfriend. Because I stood up for him, I got bullied as well.

34

Kristina: I saw a big kid hit a kindergartner. The older kid wanted some of the younger kids cards, but he wouldn't give them up. The bigger kid yelled at him using curse words then hit him. When I saw it, I told the teacher, and the big kid got in trouble. I felt proud for helping out.

Tommy: There are some kids who get constantly bullied at my school just because they aren't very athletic and don't know what to say to get it to stop. What one person I know does is ignore the bully long enough for him to go to someone else. But, if someone steals something from you, I'd tell a teacher or just take it back.

Iffer: What do you think makes kids bully other kids?

Ben: I think it's from anger that the bully takes out on other kids.

Tommy: My theory is that they see other bullies doing it, looking satisfied. They try it, but they don't feel satisfied. They want satisfaction, so they keep on bullying.

Kristina: Kids may bully other kids because they are jealous of their good grades or cool stuff.

Sophia: Also, when some kids get to the age when they become attracted to others, they don't physically hurt the person they admire, but they say things like, "You're ugly," or "You're fat."

Margaret: What can kids do if they are being bullied?

Ben: The first thing I would do if a friend were being bullied is tell a teacher. Then, if the bully kept doing the same things, I would have my friend tell the teacher about it himself, and I would try to make sure he wasn't bullied again.

Sophia: Most kids my age are bullied at school. Teachers are good people to go to for advice or to help solve a conflict. At some schools, there are conflict mediators who are older, more mature kids who solve conflicts at recess.

Tommy: When kids are bullied, they can turn the other cheek, fight back verbally, tell a teacher or leave. My advice is to take everything lightly, except when the bullying rises to the level that an adult is involved. When an adult intervenes using a deep voice, it can be even more threatening and can make the problem worse. The last thing you want to do is make an enemy.

Kristina: If kids are being bullied they should tell the person to stop!

Margaret: If you see someone else being bullied what could you do?

Sophia: Being a "Tattle Tale" is not a good idea because you can become teased even more about telling. If someone is physically being bullied, you should, of course, tell an adult who will handle the problem right away. At our age, we should be responsible enough to take care of ourselves and solve a conflict without any adult help. My class and I learned to be allies not bystanders. One time, I was made fun of because of how I looked. My friend told the person who was bulling me to bully her, too, because she had similar features. She stood up for me, and that is what being an ally means.

Tommy: When you see a person being bullied, ask for both sides of the story then tell a teacher if necessary. Or, if you feel like you have enough authority, tell the people involved to break it up .

Kristina: I agree that people should tell a teacher. Whatever you do, don't just stand there staring.

Things that Frighten Us

Margaret: Sometimes I wake up at night and am scared of the future, mostly about school and college. What are the things in life that frighten you most?

Christopher: I am scared of our house being broken into, and I am also scared about being robbed. Our neighbor was robbed at gunpoint and that made me fearful. Also, I am concerned about my grades and being able to enroll in a great college. I want to get educated so that I can have a successful life. I want to give my future family a good life, and if I don't do well in school that's not going to happen. I also want to take care of my mom and dad the best I can when they reach old age. I want to help them out like they help me now. If I don't get a great education and don't go to college, I most likely won't be able to feed a family or help my parents.

Karen: Sometimes it scares me to go outside because of all the violence out there. Our car got broken into, and I get really scared to go outside to take the trash out. I am also afraid of drug dealers on the street when I am walking in San Francisco.

Meaghan: Sometimes I am afraid of going outside when it gets dark. We have a really big back yard, and we have had two cars that have been broken into. Also, it scares me when I think of my grandma. She has cancer, and she chose to stop chemotherapy. Sometimes I wake up frightened in the middle of the night when I dream about her.

Ella: I understand what Meaghan is going through because my mom had cancer that then went away. I thought the cancer was over, but it came back. I thought she was going to die. I was hysterical. My mom is better now. Also, violence in the world is on my mind a lot, but I also think about global warming. That's something that we have to prevent, but it's very frightening to think about at times.

Malcolm: I get frightened when storms happen when I'm asleep. In the middle of a scary dream, monsters are chasing me, then I get grabbed. The lightening outside strikes, and when I wake up, I'm scared to death!

Nikki: Well, I am frightened about the future because time flies by, and you don't really know when you are going to die. I am worried that, when you get older, you will forget all of your childhood memories. The future is scary because you don't know when are you going to do things that you thought were scary when you were young. I am concerned that, when you get older, you might get more urges and do things that aren't good for your body.

Noah: The things that frighten me are scary movies that are rated R and PG-13. The scary movies are *Freddy vs. Jason, Jeepers Creepers 2, Hide and Seek, Boogeyman* and *Chucky Returns.*

Marina: One thing that frightens me is homeless people, especially the ones that smoke, and also the ones that stare. I stop breathing when I walk past people who are smoking. I also have a huge fear of snakes and spiders. They just creep me out. Sometimes I worry about the people who cut down trees. Maybe they will cut down too many, and we won't have enough oxygen.

Iffer: **To whom do you turn when you are frightened?**

Ella: I am the worrywart of the family, so when I'm afraid of something, I go to my mom. She was a worrier, too, and got frightened easily, so she knows how I feel. It helps a lot to talk to someone. Once I know I'm not the only one who's had something on my mind, I feel much better.

Nikki: Me, too. I turn to my mom because I can trust her when I am hurt. Once, when I was younger, my mom left to go somewhere, and I was scared that I would lose her.

Malcolm: Most of the time, I turn to my big brother, or, on a rare occasion, I talk with my parents. I might talk to them after I've had a scary dream. Then, after I'm finished, I don't get scared anymore.

Christopher: I always turn to my mom because she knows the right things to say to calm me down. If I can't do that, I go to my dad, and he will do the same thing. If neither of them is available, I just try to calm myself down the best that I can.

Meaghan: I usually turn to my family, my friends and sometimes even my pets. When I am sad about something that's going on at school, I talk to my family about the situation. When I'm scared about home, I tell my friends. If I'm really desperate, I go to my pets.

Marina: I'm like Meaghan. When I'm frightened, I normally turn to my friends and family, too. They help me feel better.

Noah: My parents, auntie, uncle, grandma, grandpa, and cousin. These are the people who I will turn to when I am scared.

Home

Margaret: Now that I am away at school, I value being home with my family even more. I know that for some of my friends going home is really hard, and they prefer to stay at school. What makes home special to you?

Nolan: Home is special to me because it's a place where I can relax and not have anything hanging over my head (except homework). I have always valued time at home. I feel good at home because I am comfortable, and I feel loved.

Yasmine: Home is special to me because, when I walk through the door, I smell yummy food to eat. I like having my own room so that I can put my stuff on my bed before I go to the kitchen. After I eat, I can lay on the couch while I watch some TV and take a short nap. I love my home because it is comfortable to me.

Alyssa: I like going into my room and being able to have a little time to myself. I like to have my own place to be, but I like to be with my family, too. Just a house isn't special to me. I have to be there for a while, sleep and eat there, and get used to it. I have to make it a home.

Nikki: I know what you mean. I've lived in my house for a long time, and I have gotten used to it. It is so weird how sometimes there is different weather inside the house than outside. In the winter, it is hot. When it is summer, it is cold.

Olivia: My home is special to me because I actually live in a house. It may not be the biggest house in the world, but at least I live in one. My house is great because I have a good view of the city.

Iffer: How do you feel about moving?

Darius: The hardest part of moving for me is making new friends, finding my way around, and figuring out my address.

Nikki: Well, it is hard to move because you have to pack up and unpack your stuff. Even when parents say they are not moving anymore, you do. It is useless to complain. But, looking on the bright side, you can clean up your room.

Nolan: When I moved it was difficult, mostly because I really liked the backyard at my old house. Now I have just as much fun in my current yard, but I miss the two kids on my street who I played with. I don't have any friends that live on my current street. I miss the view of the back yard from my window, and my sunny bedroom.

Olivia: If I moved, I would miss my great neighbors. Every year, my neighbors give us a Christmas present. They are always so nice to us. I would also miss my street. I love my street because the hill is fun do go down on my bike. It is also fun to go around the block with my friends. If I moved, I would really miss my house. It would just be sad for me.

Alyssa: Well, it depends on where you move. If you move really far away, you'll have to make new friends, and it will be hard to keep in touch with old friends. If you just move to the other side of the city, it will be easier because you can still see each other sometimes. No matter what, if you move, you will have to get used to the new house and neighborhood.

Yasmine: I hate moving. Packing is really not much fun. You have to name each box. It is very hard to keep track of all your stuff. Last time I moved, I lost one of my purses. Unpacking takes a lot of time, too. Sometimes it takes days to unpack if you have a lot of stuff.

Margaret: What advice would you give parents about how to make a home a place where kids will always want to return?

Nolan: In order to make a home a place a child wants to come back to, there needs to be respect in the house. There needs to be family time and laughing. The house also needs to be kept up. A home is no fun if there's junk all over, which leads me to another point. There needs to be a place to play. If there isn't, a child could get very depressed. There needs to be some social time where everyone feels comfortable just fooling around and having fun. Most importantly, there needs to be love.

Darius: Parents can give kids more choices about things they need to do.

Alyssa: I think it is important to have your own space. Even if you don't have your own room, you should still have a spot that is your own like a closet or some area you can go when you want to be alone. When I come home from school every day, I have a certain spot to do homework where everyone leaves me alone, and I can work well. It's important to have a place where you can concentrate.

Nikki: Well, if you have more than one child, make sure you have separate rooms, or the kids will get into fights like my little brother and I do. Always check on them when they are supposed to be asleep because they might be playing games.

Olivia: Parents should make home fun for their kids by spending time with them on the weekends doing things like bowling or going to the park. Then, their kids will want to come home. They can always be nicer and help their kids with homework.

Yasmine: Parents shouldn't do something that they tell you not to do. They should make time at night to sit down and share laughs with the family.

Parents

Iffer: Some of my friends' parents are fun and really easy for me to talk to, while others ask me the same boring questions over and over. What do you think parents can do to make kids want to talk with them?

Savannah: Parents are some of the most important people in a child's life. If kids aren't close to their parents, they need someone else to talk to. Kids are not born knowing everything they need to know about growing up. If parents want kids to talk to them, they should ask a few questions, then listen and not interrupt. They should not be embarrassed to talk to their child about puberty and other touchy subjects.

Isaiah: I agree, and when these touchy subjects come up, parents should also try not to change the subject or say, "I don't want to talk to you about that yet."

Campbell: I always enjoy talking to my parents. I think all kids should have conversations with their parents, and it should not be a problem for the parents. I have heard from my neighbors and friends that some of them would rather not talk to their parents though.

Alyssa: I think it helps when parents will have a laugh with me. Also, it helps if they designate a certain time to really have a conversation with me.

Yasmine: I would advise parents to give their child a welcoming present or dinner or something when their child comes home to show that they enjoy having them home. They will probably have something for their parents to show that they love them, too, and that they like being home. Home is a place all kids should enjoy.

Margaret: What do parents do to make kids not want to talk with them?

Savannah: If a child is not talking to her mom or dad, it is probably one of these reasons: 1. The parent asks the same questions every day and doesn't really listen to the answers. 2. The parent talks on the cell phone all day and gets annoyed when a child tries to talk. 3. The parent gets embarrassed when talking about certain things and discourages kids from talking about them.

Isaiah: I agree that parents ask the same questions every day. I don't want parents always talking about school and telling me not to do drugs. Also, parents should not ask just yes or no questions because that won't start a conversation.

Campbell: For other kids, if they aren't left alone enough, if their privileges are taken away or if they can't be with their friends, then they get mad at their parents, and they won't talk.

Alyssa: Sometimes if a parent doesn't talk to me at all, it makes me feel uncomfortable when we do start a conversation. Also, if they talk too much, I can't get anything out. It's hard to get enough time and enough attention to talk to a parent. When I do get a chance to have a conversation, I want to be able to get out what I have to say. It's really important to me that I get as much time to talk to my parents as possible because they can help with almost anything. Parents yelling at kids when they do something wrong is the absolute worst thing. That makes me not want to talk to parents.

Margaret: What do you wish you could talk about with your parents?

Alyssa: I wish I could tell them if I did something wrong. It is really hard to tell them because they get mad. I just have to remember that they will be even madder if I don't tell them, and they find out what I did wrong. I have to keep faith in myself and let it out.

Savannah: I can talk to my parents about anything, but I know some people can't. Some parents get all red in the face whenever their child asks them about things like puberty.

Campbell: My parents are good about talking to me. They usually don't ignore me, and there isn't anything that they refuse to talk about to me. If there were a conversation that they didn't feel comfortable talking about, they would tell me.

Isaiah: I wish my mom would talk about sports, and I wish my dad would talk about music.

Iffer: What advice have you heard too much?

Savannah: I hear, "Use common sense," a lot. I've also heard, "Don't beat up anyone," a few times, mainly as a joke. From TV, there is, "Don't eat junk food, you will get diabetes."

45

Campbell: As long as my parents know that I have been informed by a grown-up about things that they think I should know, they don't bug me about it. They don't keep telling me the same things time after time.

Alyssa: My dad always tells me how important it is to go to bed on time and get a good night's sleep. I know it's smart to get a good night's sleep, but he tells me all the time.

Isaiah: I hear, "Stay in school," way too much. My dad says, "Don't be like those kids who get into trouble, don't do drugs, and do not eat lots of fat or play video games a lot."

Iffer: What's the best advice that your parents have ever given you?

Savannah: My parents have given me a lot of good advice over the years, but the thing that sticks in my mind most is to be free. If you lose your freedom, you lose just about everything. If you get arrested, tell the police your name, nothing else. Plead not guilty. Then call them and my uncle, who is a lawyer.

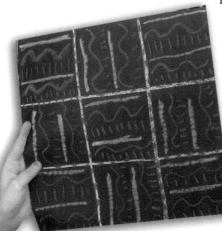

Campbell: Sometimes I feel bad for not that big of a reason. They tell me to feel good about myself and be proud of everything that I do. Also, they say not to look back on actions or decisions that I might have made. Their advice always makes me feel much better.

Alyssa: My parents always tell me that if I lie about something I did that was wrong, I will get in more trouble than telling them the truth about it. I used to get scared about telling the truth when I did something bad, but if I lied, my parents would always find out somehow. Now, I try to think about whether or not I will get in trouble, and try not to do things I will regret.

Siblings

Iffer: I realize as I grow up that my relationships with my siblings are always changing. I know that they have had a huge influence over me. What do you think are the best and worst things about having siblings?

Nikki: One thing that I hate about having siblings is that they touch my things, like homework, when I ask them not to. One thing that I like about having siblings is that I can tell them what to do since I am the oldest.

Yasmine: I agree. The worst part about having siblings is that they go in your room and mess it up. They take the covers off the bed, they put all of the pillows on the floor, and they go through my purse. My brother doesn't listen to me when I tell him to quit it. The best thing about having a sibling is that when I get in trouble, my brother tells my mother to stop. He is only four years old, and already he tries to protect me.

Campbell: I like siblings, but sometimes little sisters get on your nerves.

Nikki: Yes. But, when you are lonely, you always have someone to play with.

Alyssa: I know. The best thing about having siblings is playing with them. I have a much younger brother. I like to see him running as fast as he can when playing tag and being as quiet as he can when playing hide-and-seek. But, it's also really hard because of our eight-year age difference. I have to wait for him when he's going slowly, and

I have to try to keep him happy. Also, he does whatever I do. If I am climbing on something, he'll try to climb, too, but if he falls down and cries, who gets in trouble for it? ME! It's really hard to remember to look out for him, so I have to do the best that I can.

Nolan: The best thing about having siblings is that there is always someone to play with, someone to talk to, and someone by your side. The worst thing about younger siblings is that they mess up your stuff, snoop through your desk, hit you, bite you, etc. I am the oldest, so I am just guessing, but the worst thing about older siblings is that they get mad and hit you for no reason. They won't let you have a turn at something. They tease you, pester you, and won't let you have the TV/video remote. Or, if you have it, they'll take it from you.

Kristina: I have a younger sibling, too. My little sister just turned four, and she is the silliest sister ever with her dancing and games. My big sister is like a queen to me. She is cool and always trying to help me out. The best thing about having siblings is that you don't have to be alone. The worst is that they don't listen to you a lot, especially my little sister.

Olivia: My relationship with my siblings is definitely changing as I grow up. I used to play a lot with my brothers and sisters. Now that we are older, I really play only with my twin brother, Truman. Out of all of my siblings, I probably have the closest relationship with him. I still talk a lot to my older siblings, though. Some of them have had the same teachers, and we talk about what they had to do in that grade. One of the worst things is that I have to share a room. When you share a room, it is kind of hard to get dressed because I don't like people watching me.

Sarah: With siblings you never feel lonely. You have someone to love and care for and someone to care for you. The bad things about having siblings are the fights that you have and sharing your room or space. Sometimes your siblings invade your personal life.

Savannah: The best thing is always having someone to talk to. My brother, Max, is so funny. If you're an only child, you might get bored being the only kid in the house. The worst part is having someone to fight with all the time. I've seen some people who declare war on their little brothers and sisters, and some who hate them. It is difficult sometimes.

Iffer: Do your siblings influence your decisions?

Savannah: Yes, tremendously. I remember once I had to make an important decision that would affect a lot of people. I was about to go one way, then I thought of my brother, and I changed my mind. I knew he wouldn't like what I was going to say, and most other people wouldn't care about it.

Yasmine: My brother doesn't influence my decisions because he is only a little boy. Everything I do is okay with my brother. I don't have to ask him before I make a decision.

Campbell: Usually, my decisions have nothing to do with my siblings, but if a decision concerns them, then it matters.

Nolan: If the decision involves my sibling, I might change it to favor him. For example, he may not want me to climb up high somewhere, so I won't. Otherwise, I think for myself.

Alyssa: My brother will do almost anything I want him to do. If I say, "I feel sick," he'll bring me medicine, even if it's not the right kind. If I say, "I'm tired," he'll bring me

50

my pillow. Also, he'll copy me even if I don't want him to. Because he copies me, I have to make sure that I make good choices so that he will make good choices.

Kristina: No, my little sister does not influence my decisions. But I've learned from my big sister that I should finish college and think carefully about having a baby at a young age.

Sarah: I am an older sister. I have a little sister. I think my sister teaches me a lot behavior wise because she is much more outgoing than I was at her age. Sometimes my sister helps me come to decisions. More often, I think I influence her decisions, or at least I try my hardest to help her make the right decisions.

Margaret: What advice do you have for parents about how to treat siblings?

Olivia: My advice for parents is to treat your kids nicely. Parents should never beat up their children. My parents would never do that to my siblings and me. I also think that parents should make sure that their children listen to what they say.

Nikki: Make sure they are not lying or hitting each other. Make sure that they do their homework before they play or do anything else.

Yasmine: I would tell parents to treat their kids the same so that they don't complain. You should respect all of them.

Campbell: I don't tell my parents how to treat my sister because I think they do what is right, and it's not my decision. I would talk to my parents if I thought that they were making a mistake or if my sister were being blamed for something she did not do.

Alyssa: I know it's hard if there is a big age difference, but I think parents should try to treat siblings as fairly and equally as possible.

Nolan: No matter what, if your kids have been fighting, and you didn't see what happened, then don't fully trust either of them. They both make up stories to get the other in trouble. The rest of the time, treat them as equally as possible. Every once in a while, spend time with only one child. Go on a little outing, run an errand, anything, just spend time with one. It is important, and they need it, trust me.

Sarah: I think that each kid should be treated fairly. For example, if you have two children and you play some games with one, then you should either play with them both at the same time, get your partner to play with one or play with the second child. I think that if you are pregnant, then way before the baby is born, you should talk to your kid about the new coming baby.

Savannah: You should not treat them too differently. But if you have to, explain why to the one who isn't being favored. Otherwise that child will get mad. There would be a big scene that most parents do not want to handle. I know mine wouldn't.

Priorities

Margaret: There are times when I can't fit all the things that I want to do into the day. I have to make choices about what I value most. What are the three most important things in your life?

Christopher: Number one is definitely my family. They have always been there for me no matter what. Number two is school because it is important to my future. And, number three is sports because I like to play games.

Marina: I agree with Christopher about spending time with family and maintaining good grades. I also value friends and staying in good health, which includes exercising and eating right.

Nicholas: My family, my pets and Legos all mean a lot to me.

Truman: Reading is most definitely the number one thing. Number two, I have to say, is writing. Last, and number three, is horseback riding. It makes me so happy.

Meaghan: I do have three important things in my life, but sometimes it's a little hard to keep up with them. They are my family, pets, and school. My family is important to me because they care about me, and they love me. My pets are important to me because my pets are like siblings to me. School is important to me because without school you won't be able to succeed.

Iffer: What makes these choices important priorities?

Marina: Without these, I would not be very happy, and I wouldn't feel valuable. These three things will help me in my future

Christopher: My family is the most important thing in my whole life, and without them I would not know what to do. School is important because if I don't get good grades at school, I won't be able to go to an excellent college. And, if I don't go to an excellent college, I won't be able to get a good job, and I won't be able to feed a family. Sports are important to me because I love them, and they give me a great workout.

Truman: What makes them important is that they are all things I love to do. I read every day because I enjoy it so much. I don't care if I've read the book before. I like writing because it makes me feel like I'm getting closer to becoming an author. Then, horseback riding, how can anyone not like it? The smell is nice, and the way they canter is a really good feeling.

Iffer: What do other people tell you should be important that you don't value as much?

Nicholas: Homework, and an early bedtime.

Christopher: Nobody has really told me to value something that I don't value. I pretty much value the things in life that people who are important to me want me to value.

Darius: I think sleep is not a real value because I don't get tired in the morning, and I don't value love because I still have not been in love.

Meaghan: People tell me that I should value homework, and I do, but it just gets harder and harder.

Truman: I'm trying to value math more. This is difficult because I don't like it very much.

Marina: The majority of the things people tell me I already or mostly agree with.

Margaret: What gets in the way of spending time on the things that are the highest priority to you?

Nicholas: Homework

Christopher: I agree, it's definitely homework. When I'm finished doing homework, I can't spend any time outside playing basketball. I have an 8ft high basketball hoop that I could practice on every day, but, because of homework, I don't have time.

Meaghan: It's hard to do homework and swimming at the same time. After I swim, I have to go straight home and start my homework. Swimming usually gets in my way, but it's still really fun to swim.

Marina: Homework gets totally in the way of a lot of different things. Also, when I spend too much of my time on one of my priorities, I sometimes don't have time for the others.

Truman: I agree with everyone else about homework. When we have a lot, it cuts into my reading time. But, homework comes first before the things I like to do in my spare time.

Responsibilities

Iffer: Responsibilities range from everyday chores to doing what you believe is morally right. What are reasonable responsibilities for someone your age?

Malcolm: I think a responsibility for someone like me is taking care of my homework and doing my regular chores.

Neijah: Me, too. Getting your homework in on time is important, and eating your breakfast and cleaning your room are good responsibilities too. If you have pets, you need to make sure that you clean where they eat and sleep. That's what I have to do every day.

Sophia: Feeding and brushing my dog is an everyday responsibility. I also have to feed my tropical fish and scrub the algae off the glass. Finishing my homework and getting organized at school is a great responsibility.

Truman: I think a reasonable responsibility for children my age is being able to ride your bike around the neighborhood and to the park. My parents give my twin sister, Olivia, and me that responsibility.

Nolan: A kid my age ought to be able to stay home alone while his mom runs some 30-minute errand. Another reasonable responsibility might be helping around the house.

Meaghan: Reasonable responsibilities for kids are simple things like taking out the trash, washing dishes and clothes and cleaning your room. Now that we are getting older, we are beginning to have more responsibilities.

Iffer: What responsibilities do you think are too much to handle?

Sophia: Voting is a huge responsibility, and most kids like me cannot handle such a big responsibility. Driving is a responsibility every child wants, but I think it is just too much to handle.

Truman: I think being able to wander around the neighborhood late at night is too much to handle because we're not really responsible enough yet. Also, when you get to do that, you usually have a curfew. Kids our age won't keep track of time. All of a sudden they will notice, but it is already past their curfew. When they get home, they might get into trouble. It's just a lot to handle.

Malcolm: I think back-to-back chores like unloading the washer and dryer, then reloading the washer and dryer and folding all of the laundry are a little too much for us these days.

Nolan: Personally, I think babysitting by yourself is too big of a responsibility because kids our age can't always control little kids. Some kids may not be responsible enough to go to their rooms and just start whatever they're supposed to do when you tell them. They may start playing or something, but this does not apply to all kids.

Margaret: What responsibility do you want to take on that you are not allowed to have?

Nolan: I really can't think of a responsibility I want and can't have.

Neijah: I want more pets, but I am not allowed. I would also like to own a cell phone, but I can't have one yet. Those things would be a lot, but I could handle them.

Sophia: I would love to have the responsibility of driving and voting. Other than these, there aren't many responsibilities that I would like to have that I don't. Most responsibilities that I would like to have are too big of a challenge.

Truman: I want to be able to drive, too. It sounds really fun. Sometimes my parents let me shift gears for them, and it's cool to pull the leavers.

Malcolm: I would say I would like to try to take out the trash here and there.

Margaret: What are the best kinds of rewards for being responsible?

Truman: The best for me is getting a book. In fact, a few days ago, I went to the orthodontist, and afterwards my mom got me a book as an early birthday present.

Sophia: If I am responsible about feeding the fish and cleaning the tank, sometimes I get the privilege of buying more fish. Some of the best rewards for being responsible are just improving things that you already have. For example, if my bedtime were 8:30pm, and I was reading and managing my homework well, my bedtime would be changed to 9:00pm because my parents would trust me not to fool around at night.

Nolan: A good reward for me is a little bit of money. You know, one or two dollars, not that much, just a little something to show I did a good job.

Meaghan: I wish that I could have a TV in my room, but my parents won't let me have one because they think that I am too young. They also think that I am too addicted to it.

Neijah: The rewards I've gotten are going out to eat or getting a present. But, I would like to have a dog.

Malcolm: Obviously this is like money, but for me, I prefer going on trips to places like toy stores or video arcades.

Stereotyping

Margaret: One of my friends who is Indian has had people make comments to her about being a terrorist. She is the most peaceful person in the world, but people made a judgment about her just because of her ethnic background. Is there a time when you or someone you care about has been stereotyped?

Richard: We had a substitute teacher, and I think he stereotyped us. He treated us like we were bad kids. He was explaining the rules to us, and he said, "The most important rule is no fighting or violence." It was directed at the class in a negative way. He thought, because our school is an Oakland Public School, and there are some very bad parts of Oakland with gang violence, that we, too, were bad. We are really a great, open enrollment Oakland school.

Christopher: Being stereotyped is very discouraging. It can really hurt people and make them sad. It's never right to make fun of people just because they look different than you do. People who stereotype wouldn't be happy about it if it happened to them.

Savannah: Some people automatically think that most girls are not athletic, which isn't necessarily true. I started to take karate, and people were really surprised. They were even more surprised to learn that there were more girls in my class than boys! A lot of girls in my class at school play softball and soccer, too.

Alyssa: I am a blond, so sometimes people think I'm dumb. It makes me really mad because I know that I am really smart. People also think I'm a girly-girl because I'm blonde, but I play soccer, softball, and love hiking. Even if I were a girly-girl, it wouldn't be because I have blonde hair.

Iffer: Why do you think people stereotype others?

Christopher: People who stereotype others sometimes don't understand what they are doing to other people. They don't know what else to do, so they just start making fun of someone else. They think that they are special and can say things to people just to make them cry and feel terrible inside. Those kinds of people are probably racist.

Richard: I think people stereotype others because they have had bad relationships in the past, or they are not very well educated. Whatever the reason, it doesn't give them an excuse to stereotype.

Savannah: I think your brain automatically stereotypes some people. Television does it, too. Whenever some people see a young African American guy with baggy, sagging, low down jeans walking towards them, they cross to the other side of the road without even thinking about it. Many people would get mad about this, but it is true. I'm not saying it's right, because it's not, but it happens.

Iffer: What is the best way to fight stereotyping?

Christopher: I think you should just ignore it. If you don't show that you feel bad, people will think that their "joke" isn't working. Hopefully, they will decide to not do it again.

Richard: I think the best way to fight stereotyping is to use words and not get physical with others. Tell your teachers at school if something happens. Tell others that it is not okay to stereotype because their words and thoughts are likely wrong. They might not know that they are stereotyping and that they are being harmful to others.

Savannah: I think that if someone stereotypes you, you should do all you can, without being hurtful, to discourage them from thinking about you in that way. Sometimes it's hard to make people drop their mental image of you. Don't get too mad at them; it's not really your problem. Just try to convince them you are a good person.

Alyssa: I think a lot of the people who stereotype others feel insecure about themselves. They often think they're "cool" if they are mean, and that is how they make friends. Sometimes people don't realize they've hurt your feelings, but sometimes that is the whole point. One thing that I like to remember is that our physical features don't make up our personality.

Puberty

Iffer: When I was in middle school, the last thing that I wanted to talk about was bodies changing. Why is it so hard to talk about puberty?

Sophia: Usually when you discuss puberty, you talk about body parts, and sometimes when I hear those words, it makes me feel a little uncomfortable. Other people can be embarrassed talking about periods or wet dreams, but these things are perfectly normal, and there is nothing to be ashamed of.

Neijah: It's hard to talk about puberty because people think that it is nasty and unusual, and because bodies are changing faster than before puberty. Also, people don't know how to talk about puberty, even with people they are comfortable with.

Gabriel: I think it's hard to talk about because people have a hard time accepting the fact that bodies change. When I was about four or five, I asked my mom if I would ever change. She answered me, "Yes." I thought I would never change, but I did.

Ben: Some people say puberty is nasty, but puberty is something that you need to talk about to your family. For instance, if you are a boy it is okay to learn about girl changes. Later on, you will need to know about these changes.

Nydesha: It is probably hard to talk about puberty because people are shy, and they think that something's wrong with it, but it is very normal to talk about puberty because it is a part of growing up.

Margaret: What happens when some people develop faster than others?

Sophia: If girls do not develop as fast as others, they could be called names like "Flat Chest," which can be hurtful. Puberty usually does not have anything to do with race, but it has to do with your parents. Bras are a big deal. Some girls can become jealous of others and pretend to have chests.

Ben: If certain people begin going through changes earlier than others, people sometimes make fun of them because they are "different".

Sophia: Pimples! Many children get these obnoxious things on their faces called pimples.

Nydesha: When somebody develops faster, you shouldn't be mad or jealous because you should like yourself just how you are. Everyone is different, and people should be proud of differences.

Gabriel: It doesn't really matter when or how fast someone develops.

Neijah: When people develop faster, they probably feel uncomfortable because their friends are not going through it with them, and things are more fun with friends.

Iffer: Who can you talk to about these issues?

Sophia: In my class, my teacher teaches sex education, so I would feel comfortable talking to her. Some kids have parents who feel comfortable talking about things like that. You should always talk to someone you trust, but even though you might really trust a friend, it's not always best to tell them. I have an aunt who is very understanding and easy to talk to. She is not embarrassed talking about names of body parts or about periods.

Ben: I would go to anyone in my family to talk about this and learn from them.

Neijah: You can talk to your mom, dad, grandma, uncle and people you trust.

Nydesha: If you need someone to talk about this stuff, you should talk to someone you're very close to or you know would love to talk to you, like your mom or dad.

Gabriel: Probably your parents. But, if you don't want to, you can talk to your teacher. If all else fails, talk to someone else in your family.

Margaret: From what you have seen, what ways do you think people's priorities and values change as they go through puberty?

Sophia: When a teen gets a pimple, it's the only thing they focus on. When girls' chests begin to grow, they become interested in boys and want to show off. Same with guys if they begin to grow facial hair. Their priorities become themselves, their hair, their skin, and the opposite sex instead of school.

Ben: Sometimes they have a new voice. Everyone is going to get that someday.

Nydesha: When you go through puberty, you change in a lot of ways. You should be proud of that because you are changing from child to adult.

Gabriel: Well, I don't know how to really answer this question, but I'll try. I think people's priorities change from instead of wanting to watch TV, they want to impress the opposite sex. In ways of value, I think they wouldn't value an old teddy bear as much as they used to.

Neijah: They get cranky because they are frustrated and confused. They sometimes separate themselves from their families and friends.

Margaret: What are the biggest questions you have about going out with someone?

Sophia: Should I bring money? Should I wear something all fancy, or should I wear something casual. Should I tell my parents and will they understand?

Ben: I just want to know about her. I'd want to get a head start and figure out what she likes, etc.

Gabriel: First of all, who is this person? Second, what are this person's hobbies? Last, but not least, what are this person's parents like?

Iffer: What kinds of things should people consider before making the decision to have sex?

Neijah: Why should you? What's so good about it?

Sophia: Are you married? Can you afford to have a baby? Do you have enough money to buy clothes, diapers, food, etc.? Will your partner be responsible enough, and will you? Have you gone to college, and are you old enough? I believe that these are the most important questions. If you are not educated, then you cannot get a job and earn money. If you are not old enough, you are probably not as responsible and mature as you should be to have a child.

Nydesha: Before you even think about having sex you should make sure that you're at least older than 25. If you're any younger, you're risking really hurting yourself. You should know what you're doing.

Ben: They should know what happens to people who have sex, and what they should do if they don't want the baby. You've got to think about this.

Gabriel: Yes. I think they should consider the consequences. They could get pregnant and have a child. I think that they also should consider that they are too young.

Neijah: A person who wants to have sex should think about AIDS and other sexually transmitted diseases. People might not always tell the truth about having a sexually transmitted disease, though, so people should go to get tested with their partners.

Stress

Margaret: Trying to keep everything in my life balanced is really stressful. What are the things that cause stress in your life?

Kristina: I agree with you that trying to keep all the things in our lives balanced can be really, and I mean really, stressful. Sometimes my mom tells me to make up my bed, and, at the same time, my dad tells me to read. It stresses me out when I have to be two places at once.

Tommy: In my opinion, stress is caused by people doing something completely stupid and mean to you for no reason at all. Ranting escalates the stress.

Sarah: Doing things last minute causes me stress because there is pressure to get the project done. I take it out on my sister or mom and dad. Stress gives me a headache.

Sophia: I know. When I have a lot of challenging homework or I wait until the last minute to do something, I get stressed and nervous about finishing it on time. When I do not understand something challenging, I can become frustrated as well because I don't get it. Sometimes the person helping me gets frustrated, too!

Campbell: Being accused of something that I didn't do stresses me. Also, if I see people being picked on, I get stressed.

Nikki: When I am stressed, it is about too much homework and too many things on my mind.

Iffer: What relieves stress for you?

Sophia: I volunteer at the East Bay SPCA. When I take out the dogs there, it's like I'm having therapy. I can relax and cuddle with the puppies, and they are always so happy, which makes me happy. Screaming into my pillow also relieves stress for me. Crying isn't always a good way to relieve stress because it can sometimes be too dramatic. You should never take stress or frustration out on yourself or anyone else. When you take out your anger on someone, most of the time you get in trouble. It can also lead to a bad injury and give you a bad reputation.

Sarah: Taking breaks to have fun and play games relieves stress for me. Taking time on projects and pacing myself also relieve stress. Sometimes staying away from my sister relieves stress because she is younger, and she can be quite annoying at times.

Tommy: My advice is to scream when frustrated. Exercising is another good way to relieve stress. Acting cheerfully reduces stress for you and others.

Campbell: Often, while I am lying in bed listening to music, I feel relieved of stress. My room is quiet, and my bed is comfortable. It makes me feel relaxed.

Nikki: My mom told me how to cure stress. She said to take a long vacation, and it will clear your mind. It worked for her. One day it will work for me. For now, when I am very mad, I just scream in my pillow and try to fall asleep. Eating something delicious helps, too. Or, I go outside, sit down and read a book. If it is raining, I stay in my room for an hour.

Sarah: Everybody gets stressed at some point, and it's hard to get rid of. Relaxing activities, such as taking a bath, taking a nap, reading, watching TV and listening to music, help me when I am stressed. I just kick back and enjoy myself. When I feel better, I get back to thinking about what was bothering me. Lots of exercise and sports relieve stress, too. It helps me a lot to run out back with my dog.

Iffer: What can the grown ups in your life do to help decrease stress for you?

Sophia: Many parents pressure their kids about avoiding drugs or smoking, and this can cause stress. If my teacher could assign my class and me less homework, my stress level would go way down.

Sarah: The grownups in my life help me calm down and care for myself at stressful times. If I am stressed in math, my dad helps me solve the problem. If I have a headache from being stressed, my mom gives me medicine.

Nikki: My mom always comes in my room and tells me about happy days. For example, she'll talk about our trip to Florida. Then, she asks me if I want anything. Lots of times, she brings me chocolate cake.

Tommy: Parents, please DO NOT sugar coat ANYTHING. It makes your children feel like you are talking down to them. If your kid loses in a sport, don't say, "Good job honey, you'll do better next time." Say, "Close game, you'll play again."

Campbell: When grown-ups are polite to me, it makes me feel better. If a grown-up has already told me to do something, I like for them to wait for me to finish before they tell me to do another thing. I also feel relieved of stress when I am rewarded for something I've done well.

Kristina: One thing I do to relieve stress when I'm late for an activity is ask my mom to call the person in charge to tell them I'll be a little late.

Sports and Exercise

Margaret: After I exercise, I always feel better. I can take a run and burn off steam accumulated from a hard day. What's your favorite kind of exercise?

Tommy: Soccer is my favorite because it's nonstop. It's a good stress reliever, and it's fun for me.

Ben: Baseball! It's the best sport for me. I love playing it, and it's cooperative.

Richard: My favorite kind of exercise is playing a game like tennis. If you are mad, you can take it out on the ball and not a person. It's a fun sport, too.

Chardonnay: For me, it's jumping jacks. You use almost every part of your body. Every Monday and Thursday when we go to P.E., I always look forward to doing jumping jacks.

Olivia: I love to ride my bike. I like to ride it around the block or with my friends to the park. I want to learn how to do tricks on my bike. When I ride, I always wear a helmet for safety. It's always important to wear protection when you are playing a sport or exercising.

Ella: I like to play softball for exercise because it includes running and a chance to get better at catching and throwing. You have to think, too. I also enjoy bike riding. My friends and I ride to the park a lot. We have a great time and get a lot of exercise.

Nolan: I have two all time favorite kinds of exercise. The first is sports, mostly soccer. The second is jogging and running. I love to run. It makes me feel relaxed and joyful, but, at the same time, serious and content.

Isaiah: My favorite exercise is running because, with practice, you run faster, and it gets me in shape for all sports. I think that all kids should exercise more than once a day.

Iffer: As long as I can remember, I have been on a sports team. Being with my friends during the successes and losses of the team was my favorite part. What is the importance of team sports for kids?

Tommy: Team sports require knowing what the other players are probably going to do. It really helps your people and psychological skills. It makes team members a little bit happier in life.

Chardonnay: It is so important to play team sports because you get more fun out of exercise. You also learn new exercising and stretching techniques.

Nolan: There are many advantages to playing a team sport. I have learned that things don't always work out the way you want because other kids may have different plans. The main thing is teamwork. If you can't work with others, you're going to have a much harder life. I've learned to respect people for who they are, not for how good they are at something. I played on a really good team, then I joined a not-so-great team because my best friend was on it. After my first game, I almost burst into tears. Later, I found that, although this new team wasn't as good as my other team, they were much tighter woven. More importantly, they tried a lot harder than my other team.

Ella: When you're on a team, you work together. You have to know what to do and when, and you have to know when to back up your teammates. You learn how to not get angry when you or a teammate makes a mistake. You can learn a lot from mistakes.

Isaiah: The importance of a team is to have a great time and know that you have a specific role on the team. Sports are very fun, especially if you get the chance to play a variety of different positions. Plus, you are active, and you can lose weight.

Richard: The best part of team sports is that you get to hang out with friends. Whether you win or loose, you are always together. You should always cheer on your teammates to do their best, even if they are not good players.

Olivia: I think that it is important to enjoy what you are doing. I'm on a softball team, and a lot of times, if we lose, some of my teammates will be upset or cry. Sometimes I will get a little upset, but I try to be proud of what I do. If you pitch in a game, but you don't pitch well, you should still be proud that you got to pitch. You should also be very nice to your team. Last year a girl on my team always told people what to do. It was so annoying because she wasn't a very good pitcher either.

Margaret: One of my friends had a serious problem with anorexia. It was hard for her, but it was also hard for me to understand and accept that my friend was in trouble. Some kids diet and exercise to the point that they are unhealthy. How would you recognize if you or someone you cared about got to this point, and what would you do?

Chardonnay: I would see a change in how they act. If they used to be hyper and full-spirited, and all of a sudden they won't eat lunch or snack, then I would know. I would recommend them to a doctor so that they could go back to being healthy again. I would also make sure they ate during lunch. That's something everyone should be aware of.

Ella: If someone I knew was at that point, I would be worried. I would try to learn about it to see if I could help, but without hurting anyone's feelings. Maybe that person would see it as an issue and get help. I would check and see how my friend was doing and offer comfort. People need friends during certain times, and this would be one of them.

No Nos

Iffer: We've all heard over and over about the hazards of tobacco, drugs and alcohol, and yet we all know that there are still kids who decide to partake. What makes kids decide to drink, smoke or take drugs?

Sarah: I think a lot of kids do drugs and stuff because of pressure from others. Sometimes parents set a bad example for the kids, and the kids follow in the parents' footsteps. Another reason kids take drugs, smoke and drink is because they want to be like their friends who think it's cool. One last reason would be that the person thinks it's cool.

Ben: I don't really know why they chose to do drugs. Maybe kids smoke cigarettes because the cigarettes have nicotine in them which makes you want to do it again, and again, and again.

Christopher: I think it is the people around them smoking or drinking that makes kids want to do it. If you see your mom, dad or friends doing it all of the time, it can definitely have you thinking that it is okay and might seem cool to you. Also, if someone comes up and offers a drink or cigarette, it is hard for a lot of kids to turn it down. You might want to know what it tastes or smells like. Once you do it, you cannot seem to stop even if you know that it is very bad for your health and your friends and family.

Margaret: How can you say no when you are offered these things without feeling left out?

Ben: Well, you can say no and walk away so you don't get tempted to do it. Saying no is better than giving in.

Sarah: If friends of mine offered me drugs, alcohol or cigarettes, I would say, "NO!" If they did not think I was cool, I would get new friends. I don't think I would say "yes", even if I felt left out. I would leave so that the people offering it to me wouldn't get into my head.

Christopher: You have to think of your future if you decide to do drugs. You will get drunk or high and not able to control yourself. You have to think how drugs and alcohol might affect having a job or a family. If you are feeling left out, think about your future without drugs, and their future with them. Drugs will affect your actions in the future.

Margaret: I know that I've been at parties when friends of mine have made decisions that made me worry. What can you do if you are worried about a friend who is making decisions that might be hurtful to them?

Ben: I would talk to them and tell them what could happen. I would tell them to stop doing what ever they are doing and talk to their parents.

Sarah: You could give your friend your opinion and tell them that you're worried, but you can't force them because the final decision is theirs. You could ask an adult to help, but your friend might not want help. Sometimes, if you're really worried about your friend, you have to risk things like her getting mad or upset.

Christopher: Have them think about what they are about to do. Talk to them and make them think about the things that can get them into a whole lot of trouble and what drugs might do to their lives. But if they don't care, there is no other way I can think of that will stop them.

78

Iffer: Whom can you go to if you need help with these things?

Sarah: I would go to my mom and dad because I can trust them with everything. I know that they could help me make the right decision. If I had a friend who needed help with issues of drugs, drinking or smoking, I would tell my mom, and she would help me take care of it.

Ben: I would go to my parents and talk to them, or maybe I would go to my friends to make sure they don't do it.

Christopher: I would run to my parents. They know what to do all of the time and always know what to say. If that didn't work, I would go to a family member who could help me out.

Music

Margaret: Depending on my mood, I like lots of different kinds of music. What is your favorite kind of music?

Noah: I like jazz, hip hop, and R&B. I listen to jazz when I am relaxing. Hip hop is great for dancing and rapping.

Darius: Jazz and hip hop are alright, but, in my opinion, rap, reggae, and rock are better. I like rap because I like some of the lyrics. With reggae, I like the fast tempo. With rock, I just like the beat of the instruments.

Chardonnay: My favorite music is rap and R&B. To me, rap can be about anything, and R&B is so soulful. The feeling I get when I listen to them is just the best mood I could be in. I could be happy or sad.

Nicholas: I like jazz, classical, and rock and roll, but jazz is my true favorite. I like the rhythms and the sounds.

Richard: My favorite kind of music is rap and rock and roll because they express feelings.

Meaghan: I love rock, too. When I was seven, my brother got me interested. I've listened to rock ever since.

Olivia: Every couple of days, I switch between liking hip hop and rock because sometimes I'm more in the mood for one or the other. I play the trombone, so I kind of like the music played on a brass instrument. I've learned to play a lot of cool songs.

Nick: I guess I am the only one who doesn't have a favorite type of music. I listen to whatever comes to my mind. You don't have to have a favorite type of music. You can sing, tap or dance to any music.

Iffer: Is there a kind of music that you hate?

Nicholas: Loud music and opera.

Olivia: Yes! Opera is terrible because you can't understand the words that the singers are singing. They sing very high and it hurts my ears. When I listen to opera, it makes me want to go to sleep. Classical music makes me tired, too. Also, a lot of times, classical music is really long and I don't like long songs.

Richard: I don't like country music because it is too slow. I am the kind of guy who likes to move around a lot. Just sitting listening to country music is boring.

Darius: I don't hate any specific kind of music, but I do dislike classical and heavy metal. Also, gospel is an in-between music for me. I only like it a little.

Chardonnay: To me, all music is great. It expresses who YOU are. Listening to people's music call tell you a lot about them.

Nick: I agree. I do not have any music that I hate. I like any type of music, unless there is music playing in another language that I do not understand. Sometimes I like listening to music that is new to me or that my friends listen to like hip hop or rap.

Noah: I feel the same way. And, any kind of music that is different, I like it.

Meaghan: I don't listen to rap music very often because I don't like the bad language that rap songs somtimes have in them.

Margaret: What kind of technology would you like to have for music?

Nicholas: I like live concerts. But if I could, I would like an instrument where you could just think the notes and the instrument would play them.

Chardonnay: Or, you could have music come from your pencil when you write something down. I don't know if it's been invented yet, but it sounds cool.

Olivia: I would want to have an iPod because it comes in a lot of different colors and sizes. If you want a small iPod, then you can get the iPod Nano. If you want to watch videos, then you can get the video iPod. Plus, on an iPod, you can play games.

Darius: I would like to have a CD player. I heard on the news that a few people died because of iPods. One man died because his iPod caught on fire in his pants. I don't want an iPod, because I don't want that to happen to me.

Noah: I want an MP3 player, iPod, CD player, iPod Nano, or a Chocolate MP3 Player.

Richard: I have a video iPod. It's the best, and I really enjoy it. I wish they were a little cheaper so that all of my friends could have one.

Meaghan: I would like to have an iPod shuffle because it is fun to have portable music. Plus, iPods look easy to use.

Nick: I like my iPod because it is one of the best music players I have. Sometimes I listen to my PSP. I can play games and listen to music at the same time. They are both really good.

Iffer: Do people your age consider downloading music a problem?

Nicholas: I don't know.

Noah: I do, but some of my best friends say no because downloading costs too much money.

Nick: I agree. I think people should get free music on Limewire or other live music players. I think that it is wrong that we need to pay a dollar per song. Downloading sites should charge less.

Meaghan: I don't know anyone who has a problem downloading free music. But, music on the internet that needs to be paid for, people shouldn't take it if they don't want to pay for it.

Olivia: I think that downloading is a problem because normal CDs and songs on iTunes cost money. The money goes to the artist that sings the song that you bought. If you download the music for free, then it isn't fair to the artist because they don't get money.

Richard: Exactly. Musicians deserve to get paid for their music because they wrote it. If you go to a job and do all the work, and then the company doesn't pay you, how would you feel? I, for one, would be angry and not want to do the work anymore.

Darius: My friends and I think it's okay to upload videos but not download them. Downloading is pirating, and pirating is illegal.

Chardonnay: Well, some kids might find it a bit of a problem, but I don't. You just need to know what kind of music it is and if your parents approve of it.

TV and Video Games

Margaret: When I was younger, my mom wouldn't let me watch TV on school days. How much TV should a kid be allowed to watch per day?

Gabriel: I think kids should be able to watch as much TV as they want AFTER they've finished their homework and chores.

Nicholas: I also want to play with my pets before I do homework. As a kid, I think TV should come before homework, but my parents think the opposite.

Karen: Kids shouldn't watch TV for more than an hour and a half. I think two to three hours is too much TV. The problem is that TV is addictive.

Yasmine: I disagree. A kid should be able to watch TV for only an hour a day because the rest of the time they should be doing something to help their education.

Neijah: A kid should only be able to watch TV after their homework is done. Some people don't watch TV at all on school days. That's probably better because you don't get caught up with TV all night.

Iffer: Who should choose what TV shows or movies kids your age are allowed to watch?

Gabriel: I think parents should choose what kids watch. If kids want to see *The Texas Chainsaw Massacre* and they get their way, they will be traumatized for life.

Yasmine: I agree. Your parents should be allowed to choose what you watch because they are in charge of you until you are 18.

Neijah: It depends on who you live with or if you are with a babysitter. Your mom and dad or the responsible babysitter should choose the shows you watch. I pick the programs I watch, though, and they are not inappropriate. I only watch funny shows and cartoons.

Margaret: Some people think that violence in video games and in TV creates violence in our society. What do you think?

Olivia: I don't think kids should watch violent movies because it gives them bad ideas or nightmares.

Nicholas: I think that the violence kids watch on TV and in video games gives bullies ideas.

Ella: I agree with Nick about giving the bullies ideas. On TV, they want to get you interested by showing more violence.

Gabriel: That doesn't make sense. I don't think that a guy playing *Grand Theft Auto* is going to kill somebody five minutes later.

Karen: I think that it's true. Kids see these things and then they go out and do it. I don't think that is right. Sometimes it scares me to go outside because of all the violence. Games like that give people the wrong ideas.

Yasmine: I do think that violence in video games creates violence in society.

Neijah: That's very true, actually. I don't play video games, but some boys at my school like to play fight because of a TV show called *Narato*.

Iffer: What makes video games fun?

Gabriel: People just like to play games.

Nicholas: Being able to be a character in the game makes it fun.

Yasmine: Video games are fun because of the sound effects and the fact that that you can control them.

Neijah: People get really caught up in them, and that makes them fun.

Fun

Iffer: What's the most fun you've ever had?

Ben: I really have fun playing sports and especially playing baseball. I love playing baseball, and I'm really good at it. Basically, I have the most fun going outside.

Christopher: The most fun I've ever had was when I went to the Bahamas when I was seven. I got to go swimming and scuba diving in the sea, and I got to see all the different kinds fish there. The only thing I didn't like was that my mom and dad couldn't come the first day because my mom didn't have her ID. My sister and I went on ahead and stayed at my aunt's hotel for the first day.

Darius: The most fun I've ever had is turning obstacles into adventures because you learn a lesson at the end of your obstacles, and sometimes it's fun to learn. For example, when I had to help my mom find lobster to eat, I turned it into an adventure as I went to new places in my search. It was like being in a big forest and gathering herbs.

Gabriel: I can't really answer that question. I can't answer it because every day I'm alive is fun, and because I'm glad to be alive.

Karen: The most fun I've ever had was going to Six Flags with my friend. We stayed at least three hours, and I really liked the water slides and teacups. We had a really great time.

Sarah: I do not have a specific day that I have had the most fun in. I have fun a lot, so it's hard to say which has been most fun. I always have fun hanging out with my friends, and I do have a lot of fun at the beach.

Malcolm: When I was a year and a half old, I drove an old van down a hill and crashed into a fire hydrant. Nobody was hurt, though. That's the most fun I've ever had.

Noah: The most fun I have ever had was when I went to an arcade and played Laser Tag with friends and family on my 11th birthday. I played mini-golf in the game room, but the Laser Tag was the most fun.

Nicholas: The most fun for me is building and playing with Lego's, playing on the computer, playing with my cats, playing with my cousins, swimming, holidays, parties, going on vacations, horseback riding, visiting the pet shop and writing codes.

Margaret: If you had a free afternoon, what fun things would you plan?

Sarah: Definitely having play dates and sleepovers with friends. Also, I have a lot of fun playing soccer. I like doing art and playing with my sister and doing family activities out in the back yard. I like running around with my dog and going bike riding with my dad.

Ben: I would go out for a little time to play outside, or I would probably just chill out or play with my video games.

Malcolm: I would plan a play date with my friends, and we would have the most fun time in our lives having a water fight and playing video games.

Nicholas: I would spend it playing with my family (we have tons of games), my pets, and my Legos.

Noah: I have a lot of answers. I would say Walmart, Target, JC Penny, Best Buy, Pizza Hut, Disneyland, Great America, Six Flags, Marine World, Oakland, Vallejo, Sacramento, My Space, City Kids, Capture the Flag, football, dodgeball and that's it. Those are the places I'd go and things I would do in the afternoon.

Gabriel: I would plan to get together with friends to go to the library or play video games.

Karen: I would plan to go out to a pizza place and then go to Jamba Juice. Then, we would all go home to watch a movie and play a board game. We would stay up all night and have bacon, eggs, pancakes and grits for breakfast. We might play a few more active games at home. Then we'd go to look at puppies at the East Bay SPCA, and play with them. Last, we would all go to a park and eat lunch. Then, we would play tag until our parents came.

Christopher: I would plan to set a play date to play video games and basketball. If a friend couldn't come over, I would do those things by myself or play with my dog.

Darius: If I had a free afternoon, I would plan to go outside and ride my bike and go around the playground a few times. Then, I would go home to watch TV and play computer games for the rest of the day.

Death

Iffer: It is hard for a lot of people to talk about death. What are your thoughts?

Sophia: I am afraid to die too young! I don't want any of my loved ones to die young, either. It makes me feel so sick when I hear of killings. If I died, I would want to die in my sleep or freeze to death because I would fall asleep in the process. I would like my dead body to be respectfully cremated. I have some questions about death. Does death hurt? Do you actually go to Heaven?

Yasmine: Death is a natural process. Everyone dies sooner or later. Death is a sad process, but we have to let everybody leave at some point. Your real home is with God. You are only visiting earth for a little while.

Truman: I'm a little scared of death. A lot of people say it doesn't matter because you won't know that you are dead. Sometimes I start thinking about it, and it gives me the willies. Death also makes me kind of sad. It makes me think of my grandma who died, and I loved her a lot. It isn't always a scary thing, though. It makes more room for all the other people being born. Death can also bring back happy memories for people. I say it is scary and good.

Sarah: I know it happens to everyone, but it makes me sad to know that someone has passed away. I hope that no one dies in vain or misery and that nobody would die from cancer or murder or suicide. I want to die happy and loved, but I do not want to watch everyone I love be sad when I die. When I grow up, I do not want to watch anybody I love pass away.

Nicholas: I hate death. Death brings me to extreme sadness and despair. I lost my grandfather when I was only two years and nine months old. We did everything together. Papa Tony was my best friend. No one can ever take his place. Death has also taken many of my dear, wonderful pets. Death means awful memories. I can't say any more about it.

Malcolm: If someone in my family were to die, I wouldn't know what to do. If one of my friends were to die, I couldn't bear to look at their pale, damp, unhappy faces. It would be like time changing and death interfering with my life as if it were a toy. I would feel like a mere puppet dangling from strings, soaring down from the sky like bolts of lighting.

Nikki: I am scared about death. You never know if you will be hit by a car or if somebody is waiting for you outside. Death is an easy thing to get to. That's why you should look both ways before crossing the street. I have heard that people can come to visit you from the dead.

Isiah: My feelings about death are both good and bad because lots of people die and lots of people live. It is sad when someone dies because you no longer have a chance to get to know him or her. Your parents will always tell you about how good that person was and how smart they were. If your pet dies, you will be mad for a long time.

Gabriel: I don't want to die, EVER. But, when I think about it more, a question rears its ugly head. "What happens when you die?" But, if I don't die, I won't know the answer. So, I've decided that when I grow old, I want to die of old age, nothing else. But, that won't happen for a while. So, until then, I might as well keep on living.

Ella: Death is very hard to talk about for some people. It is something that many people wish didn't happen, although it's part of life. It is something we must accept because, if nobody died, the world would be overpopulated. The world isn't big enough, so at some point in your life, you go for a final rest. Then, it's someone else's turn to start his or her adventure and journey of Life.

Meaghan: I am afraid of death. I do not want to die. I want to be able to have a nice long life. I want to die naturally. I hope I don't die soon.

Alyssa: I agree with Meaghan. I am scared about death, too, because I really don't want to die. It gives me chills thinking about death and picturing myself dead. It also makes me sad to think about the people who I care about passing away. I don't like funerals because it makes me sad to see people crying and that makes me start to cry. Sometimes I cry because somebody I love is crying about the person they loved who died, and I don't even know the person who died.

Campbell: I do not understand death all that much. I guess that if we were born to live, then we die for the same reason. All creatures die at some point. I am not afraid of death. To me, it is completely natural.

Darius: I fear death. I think death should not exist. Death can be either painful or peaceful. I would like to have a peaceful death.

Christopher: I hate to think about death. To me, death is one of the most awful words ever. When I think about it, I think of people dying in Iraq, or about 9/11, and a lot of other terrible things. I try to stay busy, and that way I keep it out of my mind most of the time.

Chardonnay: Death is something we will all have to face one day. We weren't meant to be on this earth forever. Death can happen to anyone. It is really sad. Death can give you serious grief. I feel that, when we die, our spirits will still be here on earth, and everyone will one day come back to life.

Karen: My cousin died at a young age, so death, to me, means grief. I never want to talk about death. I know that one day we will all die, but I try not to think about it. I feel bad for anyone who dies, even if the person is not in my family. When someone I dearly love dies, I know not to blame it on myself because I have nothing to do with it.

Savannah: I think there is a reason for everyone to be on this earth, but they have to find the reason. Some people never do and waste their lives. I have a feeling that I am here to do something, to make a stir in the world. When I grow up, I do not want to be something like an accountant. I know accountants are important, but they do not make a stir in the world, really. We aren't on earth very long, so I am going to make the most of it.

Noah: I don't know much about death. I know that when people die, you do not see them anymore. My auntie died last year, and my uncle died this year. I am sad without them. I am learning in church that, if I live right and go to church, I will see them again.

Marina: I think death is dark and shadowy. It's cold and painful and makes people sad. I'm scared of death and want to be on this earth for as long as I can. Death could totally mess that up. I would be so disappointed if death got in the way of me reaching my goals. It would be nice if everyone could live a long life to 100 years old.

Tommy: My feelings about death really scare me. Will I go to some distant land of God, or will I lie emotionlessly and without thought for all eternity in a dank coffin? No one really discovers their reason for living until they are old and have already completed their life's goals. It may or may not be a pointless cycle. I think, for now, I will live life as I currently am. We shall see what happens when I die.

The Future

Iffer: What are your goals for the future?

Malcolm: One goal is to become a real dad and have a nice looking wife with two little kids and one well trained dog programmed to protect us.

Truman: In the future, I want to be very successful. First off, I want to live in a mansion. I want to go to Harvard, but not become a lawyer. I want to be very smart and finish high school and college. For my first profession, I want to be the first black President of the United States. Then, I want to retire and become a best selling author. My personal goal is to be more sympathetic.

Nolan: It is my dream to be an engineer, and it will happen. One of my personal goals is to have good handwriting. I will, hopefully, have accomplished that by the time I become an engineer. Another goal I have is to have read one hundred books by the time I get to high school.

Karen: The meaning of life is to live it while you have it. The meaning of my life is to be a striver. I was made to go for my dreams. I am here on earth because I was made to be inspirational. All human beings were made for a purpose, and mine is art.

Marina: I agree. We're here on earth to make a difference. I think the reasons that we are on this earth are to be truly alive and to value life. I hope I can make this world a better place. I will plant flowers and make plain dirt look like a flowerbed. I will invent paper (plain white and colorful) that is not made out of trees. I plan to use simple ideas for conservation throughout my life and model this for younger kids.

Isaiah: In the future, I think I will be very smart, and I will know lots about sports. In football, I will know who the best player of all time was. In baseball, I will know who hit the most home runs in one game. In basketball, I will know who the best coach was and who the best athlete was. I want to be a doctor, a football player, a baseball player or a guy that works on the news. And, I will be a spelling bee judge.

Darius: I believe that I will be involved in sports, too. I hope to be a four letter athlete like Jackie Robinson. The professional sport that I would like to play is basketball. I also think I will be rich as an athlete.

Olivia: My goal is that I finish high school and college so that I will be very well educated. One of my other goals is to play softball well enough that I can play professional softball. I will have to be very responsible because, when I move out of my house to go to college, I will have to take care of myself. I will also make sure that I stay healthy.

Richard: I don't have a clue about my future. I don't know what I will do when I am older. I'll probably find something that really interests me, and I will stick with it.

Iffer: What frightens you and what excites you about the future?

Malcolm: I am not frightened by anything in the future but my death.

Ella: I get frightened about our environment. People are trying to make a difference when it comes to pollution and other things that are unhealthy for the world, but it's still frightening. It is exciting to think about going to college, but it makes me worry about whether or not I will get in.

Nicholas: I do not really know because I am still young. I think it is fun to work on the computer, and it excites me that I could be a very good computer engineer. It would be fun. My cousin wanted to be a computer engineer, but now he is a game designer.

Savannah: I am scared about the future a lot. I worry that, when I get into middle school, I will not know what to do, and everyone else will. That would be really embarrassing. I am excited because it will be interesting and, hopefully, fun. I plan to go to college, but I have mixed feelings about it. One half of me really wants to go new places and do new things, and the other half wants to stay at home, especially since we are moving this year to a different country.

Olivia: I feel the same way. I am worried that I might get lost going to my classes, but I'm also excited about going in to middle school because I will get to meet a lot of new friends.

Neijah: The things that excite me are getting a good job and going to college.

Darius: I am excited about the future because I might go to college. Nothing really frightens me about it because I'm heading in a good direction now. I'm working hard, so I don't have anything to fear about the future.

Sarah: It frightens me that there's a chance my future will be unsuccessful. I am excited to grow up and learn and fulfill my dreams of becoming an actress or a doctor. I am scared to move on to middle school and high school.

Margaret: What are your hopes for your future?

Savannah: I hope to go to UC Davis or someplace in Australia for college and get a PhD. Then, I think I want to go to veterinary school. After that, I want to travel around the world and, maybe, go into space. I might possibly be President or an artist. I want to have three kids, twenty hamsters, five dogs, five cats and lots of rabbits, birds and guinea pigs. People might think that I'm not able to do things as well as other people because I am a girl. I know there are people like that. Also, I worry that going to college costs a lot of money. I might try to get a scholarship. It is hard to get into vet school, but I know my family will support and help me.

Ella: I want to become a lawyer and go to court. I don't want to deal with murders, but with things more like financial situations. I also love acting and hope to pursue it.

Nicholas: I hope my friends will still be my friends because they are the best to me. They play with me and help me with homework.

Neijah: My hopes are to help sick children get better, maybe be a doctor. I'm not having any kids. That just seems like too much.

Olivia: I will graduate from high school and college. Then, I hope that I will become a professional softball player and be an Olympic champion. I also want to have a family, but still play softball. I want to continue to have the friends that I have already. The future will be fun!

Sarah: I hope to fulfill all my dreams and become something I will be proud of. I will go to college and keep opportunity open. I hope to have a caring and loving family by my side. I hope always to be nice and friendly and have loving friends to help me through transitions. I hope I am not a failure or a disbeliever because I can do anything I wish, if I set my mind to it.

Darius: My hopes for the future are to go to a good college, have kids and get a wife. What would get in my way are bad grades. I am trying to raise my grades now.

Malcolm: I wish to be a great winner and have a huge, good life. First, you have to get through school. My disturbing friends will get in the way, but I will just ignore them, do my work and stay on task.

Iffer: What will it take to get there?

Nicholas: It will take all my effort to get where I want to be, so I'll try my best. One thing that might get in my way is doing badly at something.

Olivia: I think that I will have to work hard and keep getting good grades to get into a good college. I don't want to go to Harvard, but I want to go to a good college. If I want to be a softball player, then I will have to work hard on softball. The future will be fun, but it will take responsibility. I will try to do the best I can.

Savannah: It will definitely take a lot of hard work and lots of homework. I don't think I like the idea of that, but it will work out in the long run.

Ella: Reaching my goals will take concentration, no distractions and friends to make me happy and keep up my confidence and enthusiasm about getting to my goals. If you don't think you can reach your goals, your friends always talk to you about not giving up and make you feel better.

Sarah: I will work hard and study hard, so I can fulfill my hopes and dreams. I will work hard through the fifth grade; I will work hard through middle school; I will work hard through high school and college. I will try my best to succeed!

Meet the Authors

| Campbell | Christopher | Darius | Benjamin | Nick | Malcolm | Nolan |

| Gabriel | Truman | Tommy | Nicholas | Richard | Noah | Isaiah |

| Alyssa | Chardonnay | Ella | Karen | Kristina | Marina | Meaghan |

| Nydesha | Neijah | Nikki | Sophia | Olivia | Savannah | Sarah | Yasmine |